by Judith Herbst

 Lerner Books • London • New York • Minneapolis

First Published in the United Kingdom in 2009 by
Lerner Books,
Dalton House,
60 Windsor Avenue,
London SW19 2RR

Website address: www.lernerbooks.co.uk

This book was updated and edited for UK publication by Discovery Books Ltd.,
First Floor, 2 College Street, Ludlow, Shropshire SY8 1AN

British Library Cataloguing in Publication Data
Herbst, Judith
  Aliens. - 2nd ed. - (The unexplained)
  1. Human-alien encounters - Juvenile literature 2. Life on
  other planets - Juvenile literature
  I. Title
  001.9'42

ISBN-13: 978 0 7613 4306 6

Printed in Singapore

Table of Contents

'There's no use trying,'
Alice said.
'One can't believe
impossible things.'

'I daresay you
haven't had much practise,'
said the Queen.

– Lewis Carroll, *Through the Looking Glass*

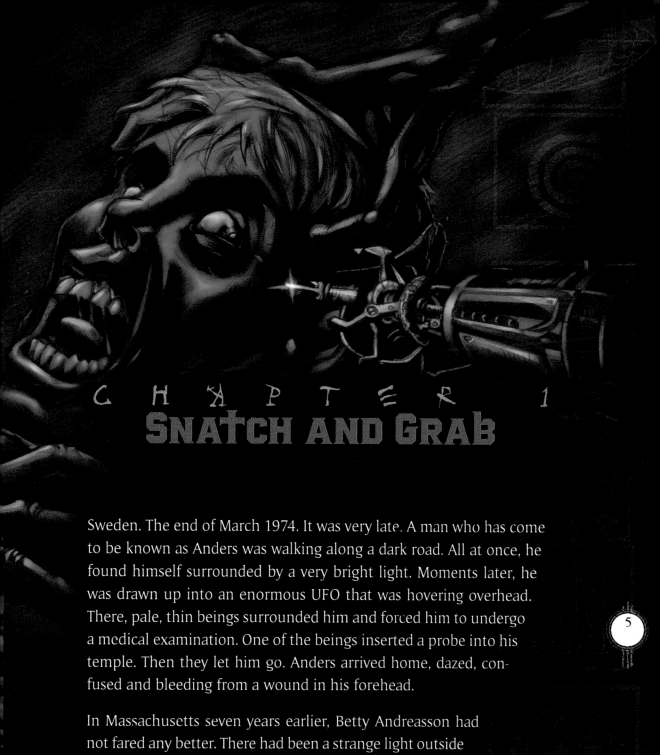

SNATCH AND GRAB

Sweden. The end of March 1974. It was very late. A man who has come to be known as Anders was walking along a dark road. All at once, he found himself surrounded by a very bright light. Moments later, he was drawn up into an enormous UFO that was hovering overhead. There, pale, thin beings surrounded him and forced him to undergo a medical examination. One of the beings inserted a probe into his temple. Then they let him go. Anders arrived home, dazed, confused and bleeding from a wound in his forehead.

In Massachusetts seven years earlier, Betty Andreasson had not fared any better. There had been a strange light outside the house, she said. Her father could see it shining brightly through the kitchen window. He looked out. There were creatures in the back garden. As Betty watched, the creatures began entering the house through the wall. She was abducted and taken aboard a UFO, where she was given a physical examination. A probe was inserted into her navel while a creature who told her his name was Quazgaa looked on. She was brought to another room and submerged in some kind of liquid. Then she was 'floated' over a 'crystal city'. Eventually, she was released. Betty said the aliens had given her a thin book, but she had lost it.

Does this seem strange yet? Here's another one.

Amilton Vierira photographed an immensely bright light over the city of São Paulo, Brazil, in 1984. Some people thought it was a UFO.

On the night of 17 October 1973, police officers came to the aid of a man stopped on a motorway between Alabama and Florida. The man reported that his pickup truck had been attacked.

The officers blinked. Attacked? Attacked how?

By an object, said the man. A UFO. It had sucked him right up.

The man claimed to have been examined by six small beings inside the UFO. The officers nodded. What could they say? The man seemed to be sincere and no, he hadn't been drinking. They filed a report.

Okay. One more, and this is a winner. In November of 1987, Ed Walters spotted a UFO and ran to get his Polaroid camera. As the camera whirred and took picture after picture, a beam of blue light shot out from the underside of the craft, paralyzing Walters. The beam then drew the motionless Walters into the UFO, mysteriously depositing him in his garden some time later.

For the next six months, Walters felt as if he was being stalked. The UFO returned again and again, sometimes chasing him with its blue beam. Once a creature of some sort crept close to Walters' house, but Walters wasn't able to photograph it. He did draw it, though.

Walters complained of a buzzing in his head every time the UFO was near. Some people believe the buzzing was due to a homing device that the aliens had planted in his brain. However, just before Walters was scheduled to undergo a CAT scan to find out for sure, he was abducted again. After that, the buzzing stopped. Obviously, say his supporters, the aliens removed the implant before it could be discovered.

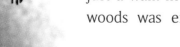

HOW TO FAKE A UFO

First, build a model. (UFO kits are available.) Next, take a photo of an interesting place. This will be your background. Find out where the sun was when you took your photo. You will need to know this so you can adjust the lighting on your model. Next, photograph your UFO against a large piece of green cloth that is lit evenly from behind. Finally. . . . Well, that's enough instruction. The last thing we need is another fake UFO.

By May of 1988, it was all over. Walters had taken several sharp photographs of what looks like a real flying saucer – no strings attached. However, a great deal of controversy swirls around this story, as well it should. In fact, just about every abduction story sounds like the plot of a poorly-made science fiction film. So you have to ask yourself, are these people making it all up? Are they crazy? Or were they really abducted by aliens? Let's see if we can work it out.

≫ Betty and Barney Get Abducted

Reports of alien abductions are not new. For centuries, people have feared being kidnapped by strange beings. Legends tell of ogres, dwarfs, giants, leprechauns, goblins and all kinds of evil spirits carrying off children while they slept. Sometimes just a walk in the wrong part of the woods was enough to put you in

An illustration from the 1880s book *British Goblins* shows fairies carrying off a baby.

danger of being kidnapped. But those creatures were all make-believe, right? Some people didn't think so.

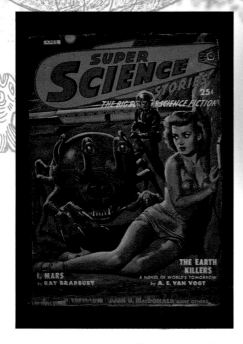

A bug-eyed alien ogles a beautiful Earth woman on the cover of this *Super Science Stories* magazine.

The science fiction magazines of the 1930s and 1940s did a great deal to popularize aliens. In issue after issue, heroes and damsels in distress were carried off by big, bug-eyed monsters, things with tentacles and big-brained beings from *out there.* Once Hollywood had mastered the art of molding latex into aliens, film makers had a field day scaring audiences. By the 1950s, it was all coming together: magazines, films and a host of UFO sightings. The public had been primed. They were ready for a real abduction.

It happened – or at least it appeared to happen – in September of 1961. Betty and Barney Hill were on their way home to New Hampshire, USA, from a holiday in Canada. It was late at night. Barney was driving. All at once, the Hills noticed a very bright light just ahead of them in the sky. Betty kept watching and remarked that the light seemed to be keeping pace with the car. Moments later, she told Barney she thought that it was getting closer.

Barney pulled over, turned off the car's engine and got out. The light had dropped down and was level with the trees.

Barney Hill shows off an illustration of the UFO he and his wife, Betty *(left)*, saw one night in 1961.

Betty grabbed a pair of binoculars and saw that the light was coming from some kind of vehicle. She handed the binoculars to Barney so he could see for himself. Barney started to walk towards the vehicle and then suddenly froze. There were odd creatures inside! They were staring at him through the windows! Panicked, Barney raced back to the car and they drove off. But when the Hills arrived home, they realized they had somehow 'lost' two hours. What could account for all that missing time? Where had they been?

The following day, Betty called her sister and told her the whole story.

'You know,' said her sister, 'you and Barney might have got a dose of radiation from the UFO.'

Oh, gosh! Did she really think so?

Well, yes. It was certainly possible. And the effects could be . . . well, you know.

Betty didn't know. So she decided to go to the library and find out. Unfortunately, the book she selected was *The Flying Saucer Conspiracy* by Donald Kehoe. Kehoe believed that UFOs were extraterrestrial spacecraft and, after reading his book, so did Betty. A week later, she had a nightmare in which she and Barney were abducted by aliens.

Two years passed. Barney, who suffered from high blood pressure and ulcers, was barely sleeping. He felt miserable and decided to see a doctor. The doctor recommended that Barney consult a psychiatrist. Betty, meanwhile, continued to read UFO books and have nightmares. She often dreamed of being abducted by aliens and forced to undergo physical examinations. The dreams left her tense and anxious. Soon she began to wonder if something else might have happened on that night in September. There had been those two hours of missing time. . . . She decided to go along to the psychiatrist with Barney.

≫ Betty and Barney Get Hypnotized

In 1963 Dr Benjamin Simon hypnotized the Hills. In separate sessions, Dr Simon asked Betty and Barney to describe their experience with the UFO. Barney was a little vague about the abduction and disagreed with Betty on a

Dr Benjamin Simon

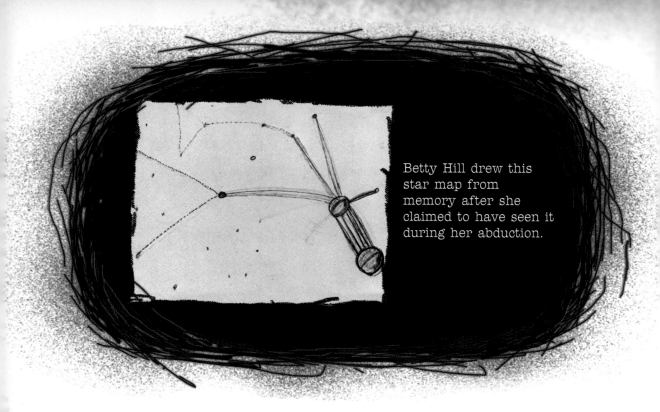

Betty Hill drew this star map from memory after she claimed to have seen it during her abduction.

number of details. Betty's story, however, was astonishing. They had been stopped by the UFO, she said. The beings had forced them out of their car and taken them aboard the spacecraft. She and Barney were placed on a table and given a physical examination. Hair and skin samples were taken. A needle was inserted into Betty's stomach. It had been horrible! Humiliating! At last, they had been let go.

Was that all?

Well, there was one other thing. Betty said she had seen a map while she was on board the UFO. It was a star map. Afterwards, she had been able to draw it quite accurately.

Dr Simon felt certain that Betty's story was fantasy. Betty had spent nearly two years reading UFO books. She had been dreaming about being abducted. So when Dr Simon asked Betty under hypnosis what had happened to her, Betty had several sources from which she could draw. Her brain simply put together whatever seemed reasonable.

Barney's story did not match Betty's, but it was similar. This was probably because Betty had often shared her dreams with Barney. Over and over, Barney had heard the details of his wife's night-time 'abductions'. When Dr Simon asked him to describe his experience, he did what Betty did. He wove together bits and pieces of what Betty had told him with fillers from his own imagination. This is called confabulation.

So the Betty and Barney Hill 'abduction' was a non-event and it would have disappeared quietly, except for two things. The first was John Fuller's book *The Interrupted Journey*, which told the story of the Hills'

Betty and Barney Hill pose with *The Interrupted Journey*, a book based upon their accounts of being abducted by aliens.

extraordinary – not to mention fictional – adventure. Then there was the star map Betty had drawn.

≫ Betty and Barney – The Legend Continues

The Interrupted Journey came out in 1966. In 1969, a teacher, named Marjorie Fish made a three-dimensional version of Betty's star map. Fish, who had swallowed the Hill story hook, line and sinker, hoped to identify the aliens' home star. And she did. The aliens, she announced with confidence, had come from a double-star system in the Southern Hemisphere constellation Reticulum. Isn't that interesting?

In 1975 the made-for-TV film *The UFO Incident* aired on American TV. The Betty and Barney Hill story had become legend. Sadly, the publicity and media hype only served to cement the Hills' belief that they had been abducted. Barney, in fact, said, 'I wish I could think that it was just a hallucination....But all these things did happen to me.' We can talk ourselves into anything.

GEORGE AND THE VENUSIANS

Hamburger stand owner George Adamski was anxious to see a flying saucer. After making several trips into the California desert, he finally got lucky. Adamski's saucer was big and silvery and when it landed, a humanoid alien emerged and told Adamski that he was from Venus. Adamski snapped a photo of the ship and, as a result, he was on many TV programmes – a lot more fun than selling hamburgers.

The Betty and Barney Hill case opened the floodgates to a rush of alien abductions. People everywhere were staggering out of

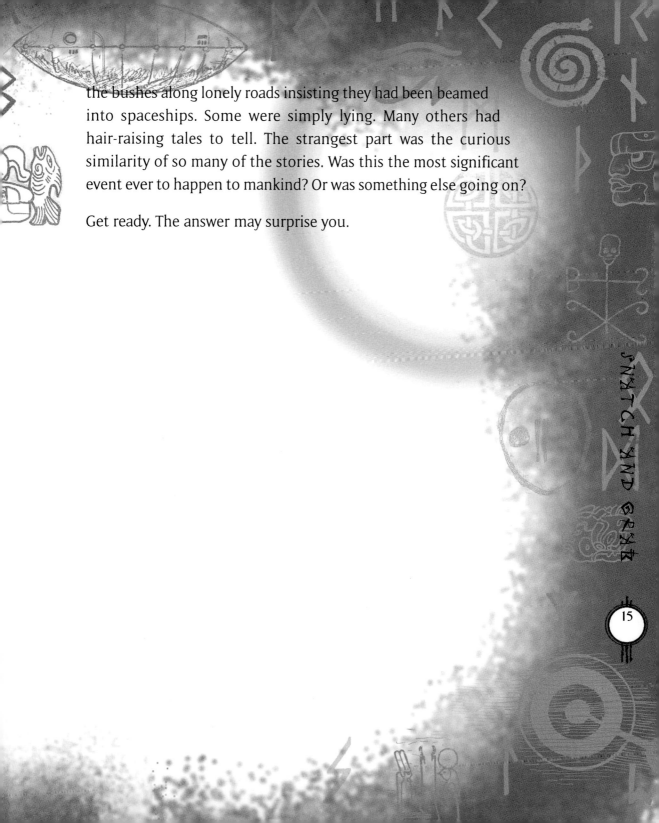

the bushes along lonely roads insisting they had been beamed into spaceships. Some were simply lying. Many others had hair-raising tales to tell. The strangest part was the curious similarity of so many of the stories. Was this the most significant event ever to happen to mankind? Or was something else going on?

Get ready. The answer may surprise you.

CHAPTER 2
YOU ARE GETTING VER-R-RY SLEEPY (AND CONFUSED)

There's no doubt about it. Being dragged into a spaceship by creatures from another planet would be a very scary adventure. In fact, it would be so awful that you'd probably want to forget the whole thing. And you might be able to. Sometimes the mind can 'bury' experiences that are too painful to remember. This is called repression. Repressed memories are hidden away in the subconscious, where they hang like underwater mines. Probe deep enough in just the right spot and boom!

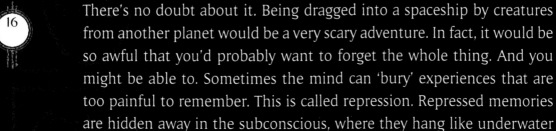

After the Hill case, abduction researchers who didn't bother to read the fine print decided that hypnosis would be the key to alien city. It would neatly and cleanly unlock all those repressed memories with one wave of a pocket watch. Why, there might be hundreds – no, thousands – of people who had been snatched and didn't even know it. Magical, mystical hypnosis would get at the truth. It would set everybody free.

It sounded like a great idea, but only to those who didn't really know much about hypnosis. They thought they did, though. So, misinformed

Facing page: Subjects are able to perform seemingly unnatural acts while in the very mentally relaxed state induced by hypnosis. *Below:* A hypnosis session

Wanted: Abductees

Not long ago, psychologist Susan Clancy set out to find people who'd been abducted by aliens. No, she wasn't planning a reunion. Dr Clancy believes that people can have memories of events that never happened. They've either forgotten how they acquired a particular memory, or their memory is faulty or has become distorted. Dr Clancy's abductees seemed to like their abduction memories. The aliens, they said, had given them a sense of belonging.

and hoping for a breakthrough, self-styled researchers invited everyone who thought they had been abducted to come on in and be hypnotized. And lo and behold! The abduction tales flowed like rushing streams.

Curiously enough, some of the people were actually relieved to find out they'd been abducted. They had suspected it, they said. Now they knew why they'd always been afraid of the dark, of needles, of bright lights. It explained all those strange dreams they'd been having. When they were children, they'd checked under the bed for monsters. Of course! They were looking for the aliens! The nosebleeds they sometimes got, the unexplained bruises. At last the pieces were falling into place. The truth was out. They'd been abducted!

Then again, perhaps not.

≫ Story Time

Even though hypnosis has been practiced for thousands of years, nobody is sure what it is that's being practised. The word *hypnosis* comes from Hypnos, the Greek god of sleep, but hypnosis isn't sleep. In fact, the last thing the hypnotist wants is a sleeping subject. Sleeping subjects can't respond and responding lies at the heart of hypnosis.

In George Du Maurier's 1894 novel *Trilby*, the domineering hypnotist Svengali transformed a tone-deaf woman into a brilliant singer.

Hypnosis has also been called an altered state of consciousness, but it's not that either. There's nothing altered about a subject's consciousness. He or she is very relaxed, but that's about it. Hypnosis isn't meditation, since the object of meditation is to free the mind of all thoughts. Under hypnosis, the subject is specifically asked to think. Think back; think forwards; think about a place; think about the scene of the crime; think, think, think and remember. The hypnotized mind is very active. The meditating mind is passive, stilled and quieted.

And contrary to popular belief, hypnosis is not a trance. In old black-and-white films, the evil Dr Demento wiggles his fingers at the lovely Daphne and tells her that she is in his power. Her eyes close and she nods dumbly. Later on in the film, she is seen walking around like a zombie, carrying out a mission for Dr Demento. Fortunately, this isn't hypnosis either. It's Hollywood nonsense.

19

An actor, arms outstretched towards his subject, portrays a hypnotist in typical Hollywood fashion.

What, then, *is* hypnosis? As far as we can understand, hypnosis is not much of anything. All the hypnotist does is encourage the person to relax. Imagine yourself on a warm beach. The sand is warm. The sun is warm. The breezes are light and soothing. The waves are lapping gently against the shore. Go with the image. Get into the scene. People do. Well, most people do.

You may have heard that some people can't be hypnotized. This is true, but mostly because they don't want to. If you resist, if you sit there with your teeth clenched and a sour look of resolve on your face, no, you will not be hypnotized. How can you relax if you're clenching? You have to trust the hypnotist and be willing – eager, even – to play along. This is just how alleged abductees feel when they show up to be hypnotized. They aren't chosen at random, the way telemarketers randomly dial phone numbers. These are people who, for one reason or another, suspect they might have had a too-close-for-comfort encounter.

When word got out – thanks to the book he wrote – that artist and UFO 'researcher' Budd Hopkins was using hypnosis to identify abduction victims, scores of worried people wrote to him. 'Hypnotize me! I think I have been kidnapped by aliens!' You couldn't ask for better subjects.

Well, yes, but that shouldn't matter. Even If someone shows up leaning towards particular beliefs, nobody can lie under hypnosis, right?

Wrong! We have all been led to believe that hypnosis is some sort of truth serum, but this is a myth. Hypnosis only *seems* like a straightforward question-and-answer session.

    – Did you see the UFO?
    – Yes.
    – What did it look like?
    – It was disc shaped, with a row of red lights.

Little by little, the hypnotist's questions draw out the story. Through the mysterious power of hypnosis, the subject must tell the truth. That's the fictional version anyway. In reality, hypnosis is more like a game that's played out between the hypnotist and the subject. The object is simply to please the hypnotist by answering his or her questions. There's no rule that says you can't invent things.

So the hypnotist says:

– Tell me about the UFO. What did it look like?

The person may have seen only a strange light in the sky. So you'd be likely to get this for a response:

– It was very bright.

So far, that would be the truth. It would reflect what the person actually saw. However, if the hypnotist pushes the person for a more detailed description, the game, as they say, is afoot!

– What was it shaped like? Was it a disc?
– Yes. (A disc? Yes. Why not? Let's make it a disc.)
– Did you see any windows?
– Yes. (Windows! Hey, that's a good idea.)
– How many?
– Four. (Four seems reasonable.)

So it goes on, until the subject has spun a fantastic tale of an abduction that never took place. This, as we mentioned, is called confabulation. The hypnotized person is not consciously lying or even trying to mislead the hypnotist. He or she is simply attempting to answer the hypnotist's questions. If the subject can make up parts of the story, the hypnotist can rig the session.

People are very suggestible under hypnosis. That's why stage hypnotists can get members of the audience to cluck like chickens and pretend they're laying eggs. So it's possible for a biased hypnotist to 'load' the questions. 'Can you describe the UFO?' certainly sounds innocent, but the hypnotist has just introduced the term *UFO*. What the subject saw is no longer a light.

It's been labelled. Now it's a UFO. A new idea has been planted in the subject's mind and the subject begins to build on it. Hypnotists who personally believe that people are being abducted can introduce all kinds of suggestions without realizing it. Even hypnotists who have no opinions on the subject or think it's all nonsense can influence the subject. And, oh boy! The tall tales will fly!

>> Creature Features

Dr Simon suspected that the Hills were confabulating. In most cases, though, the hypnotist can't tell when the subject is filling in the blanks with details from other sources. The only way to be really sure is to check out the subject's story. That's almost impossible to do when it comes to abductions.

In his book *Missing Time,* Budd Hopkins describes the adventures of 37 people who came to him, were hypnotized and walked home thinking they had been abducted. Psychiatrist John Mack has also hypnotized a number of people who related weird abduction tales. Were all these people confabulating? Abduction researchers insist they were not. How do they know? Simple, say the researchers. The stories are all strikingly similar. They contain the same elements.

Budd Hopkins

Many of the victims awoke in the middle of the night to find one or more creatures in the room with them. Others had seen a UFO

Psychiatrist John Mack used hypnosis on more than one hundred subjects who felt they had experienced alien abductions.

while driving and had stopped the car to get a better look. The creatures were most often described as thin, greyish in colour, with huge heads and enormous eyes. The victims were moved through walls or lifted into the UFO on a beam of light. Many were given medical examinations, which left scars. Afterwards, few could remember anything about their abduction, but most reported 'missing time'.

So, say the believers, how is it possible for so many people who don't know each other to make up the same fantastic experience?

For one thing, our imagination is a lot better than we think – especially under hypnosis. Hypnosis seems to allow the mind to roam freely, to help itself to thoughts and ideas. Is it magic? No. It's just a very relaxed mind that has been given permission to tell a story. And the stories are alike because everyone has been exposed to the same source material. Books, films, tabloid newspaper stories and TV all tell us what aliens are supposed to look like. Do they really look like this? Who knows? It's hard to imagine nature choosing such a rubbish design.

There is a major structural problem when you plonk a gigantic head onto a thin body and an even thinner neck. Heads weigh a lot. That's why we have so many muscles in our necks. Unless these big-headed aliens have

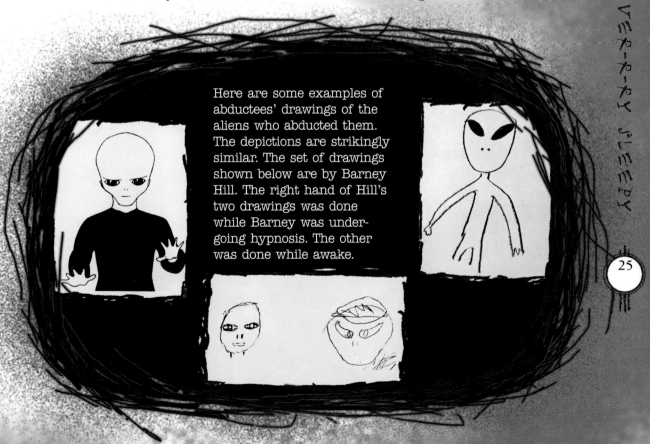

Here are some examples of abductees' drawings of the aliens who abducted them. The depictions are strikingly similar. The set of drawings shown below are by Barney Hill. The right hand of Hill's two drawings was done while Barney was under-going hypnosis. The other was done while awake.

An artist's rendition of an alien, showing the large head and almond-shaped eyes typically noted in abductees' descriptions.

steel rods in their necks, they won't be able to hold up a head that is often depicted as being wider than their torso. Even creatures from outer space have to develop according to the laws of physics.

Psychiatrists will tell you that plenty of genuine repressed memories come out through hypnosis. But they are quick to add that hypnosis can also plant false memories. And a biased hypnotist will easily find what he or she is looking for, especially when all the subjects are more than willing to cooperate.

Psychologist Robert Baker tells how the Amazing Kreskin hypnotized 14 people on TV and gave them a posthypnotic suggestion. They would all be going outside afterwards, he said and when he dropped his handkerchief, everyone would see three flying saucers. Not only did the subjects see the imaginary saucers, they described them in great detail. We can only wonder what might have happened if Kreskin had suggested the subjects had been abducted!

Clearly, hypnosis has too many 'truth' loopholes to make it a reliable method for investigating abductions, but hypnosis is not always needed. Plenty of people remember their experience quite clearly. No, they insist, it was not a dream. Or was it?

YOU ARE GETTING VER-R-RY SLEEEPY

C H A P T E R   3
WAKE UP
AND SEE THE ALIENS

Sally was six when the nightmares started. Images of great, dark UFOs filled her dreams. Sometimes she would find herself on one of the ships, surrounded by little creatures. Once, an 'alien girl with no hair and a red bow on her head' peered through the bedroom window and invited Sally to come out and play. Sally followed, and the red-bowed alien led her to a spaceship, offering her a tour. Like her mother, Jerry, Sally believes she has been abducted by aliens. Her night-time adventures are too real to be dreams.

Catherine sometimes wakes up paralyzed. A creature 'of some kind' is in the room, standing behind her. She can't see it, but she can feel its presence. Suddenly, the creature grabs her. Its long, cool fingers end in bulges, like the toes of a tree frog. Catherine tries to scream, but she can't. She also has dreams in which she is in a space-ship with curved walls. She thinks she has been abducted.

Whitley Strieber, an author of occult fiction, claims he has been visited by aliens since the mid-1980s. He says he awakens in the depths of the night to see creatures with flattened faces and black, glossy eyes. They have entered his house through the walls. They lead him away, erase his memories, plant thoughts in his head, stick needles into him and bother him relentlessly. Strieber admits the encounters terrify him, but he has accepted his fate. He believes the 'visitors', as he calls them, are here for a reason. As his adventures continue, Strieber feels he, along with the rest of us, will come to understand the visitors' purpose. No, he is not crazy and he insists, these are not dreams. Surely he can tell the differ-ence between a dream and reality. We can all tell the difference, can't we? Well, sometimes perhaps not.

>> The Night Fantastic

Almost everyone has had a nightmare. It is a dream that scares us. We wake up sweating, our heart pounding. We feel disoriented and the unsettling effects linger throughout the day. In myths and folklore, the nightmare is an evil being, an old hag who silently enters the bedroom and climbs up onto the chest of the unsuspecting sleeper. Her presence brings frightening dreams and a

though it is. You try to move, but you can't. You will yourself to throw back the covers. Come on, come on, come on. But you continue to lie there, paralyzed, watching, curious. The creature and the man have an evil intent, but they do not approach the bed. Then something begins to pull you back. You close your eyes and sleep surrounds you. . . .

In the morning you wonder. . . . I heard a noise. The telephone. Did it ring? Someone was in the bedroom. No, right outside the window, looking in. You shake your head. That's impossible. It must have been a dream, but it wasn't like a regular dream. I was awake. It was real. You shake your head again, as if to clear it. Logic assures you that whatever you saw came from your own mind.

DOES THE WORD 'HOAX' SPRING TO MIND?

Late one November night in 1989, the aliens visited Linda Cortile. They transported her through the closed window of her 12th-floor flat and into their hovering UFO. In letters and tape recordings to Budd Hopkins, two policemen named 'Richard' and 'Dan' claimed to have witnessed the abduction from their patrol car. But 'Richard' and 'Dan' never came forwards and Linda's husband slept through the whole thing.

Some people don't think so. To them, the incredible actually occurred. Creatures were standing in their room, creatures with glossy eyes and long, thin fingers. They oozed through the walls like a ghost, while their spaceship hovered just above the trees outside. No one else saw the UFO and its cobalt blue beam. The cat at the foot of the bed did not stir. Husbands and wives slept peacefully beside them, unaware that their spouse had been paralyzed by aliens and then beamed up to a waiting ship. The imagery was so vivid, the sense of reality so powerful, it had to have happened.

What's so amazing about all of this is people's willingness to embrace several truly fantastic ideas. They'd rather believe they were abducted by aliens under everybody's nose than consider the possibility that it was a hypnagogic hallucination. Perhaps it's because we often associate the word *hallucination* with mental illness. However,

C H A P T E R 4
WHY US?

No wonder the aliens keep coming back. Our planet is a nice place to visit. Plants and animals in abundance. Lots of water. A terrific atmosphere full of oxygen. And you couldn't ask for a better pull of gravity. However, Earth is a dark ball of rock. Even through the most powerful telescopes, it is invisible from outside the solar system. So if there really are aliens here, how did they find us? With the exception of a few modest radio signals, we don't advertise our presence. To pick up our feeble radio waves, alien receivers would have to be aiming in our direction and the odds of that are, well, astronomical. Let's assume they got lucky and managed to pinpoint our location. Aside from our breathtaking views, what makes us so interesting? It can't be our super-advanced science. The aliens are the ones with the interstellar rockets. So what do they want from us?

Over the past two decades, abductees have practically been coming out of the woodwork. In fact, according to psychiatrist John Mack, surveys have suggested that as many as a million people in the United

UFO abductee Bruce May shows photos of himself with scars on his shoulder. He believes the marks are evidence of experiments performed on him during his abduction by aliens.

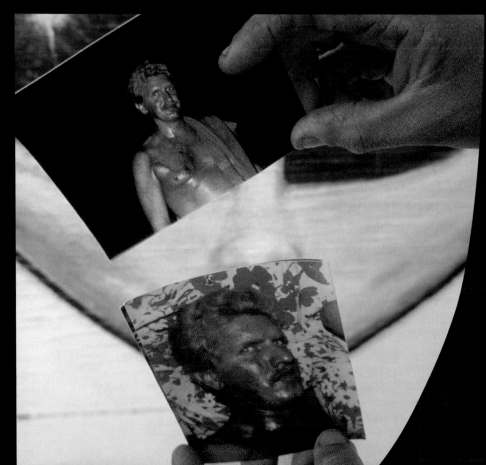

HAVE YOU HEARD WHAT'S UNDER DULCE?

Dulce, New Mexico, USA, is a little town with a very big population. Most of it, however, is underground. According to the rumours, 18,000 aliens are hiding beneath the pavements of Dulce. This particular group are the Greys, so named for their distinctive colour. The Greys aren't trespassing, though. They were born here long, long ago but have forsaken their home and become agents of the Draco, a bad group of reptiles who have turned an asteroid into a spaceship and are heading to Earth.

The aliens living under Mount Shasta in California, USA, are also natives, having descended from the Lemurians. (Lemur, like Atlantis, was a continent supposedly swallowed up by the sea.) The Mount Shasta entities are generally friendly towards humans. The aliens seem to be everywhere, don't they? Perhaps they need to start paying taxes.

amoeba. So how much of a mystery can our biology be, especially after they've supposedly examined several thousand of us? What can a poke in the leg tell them? High school biology students do not poke frogs in the leg to find out what's inside. They dissect them!

42

A small percentage of abductees believe the aliens put something in their brain, such as a tracking device. They remember a needle being inserted into their temple or between their eyes. For several weeks after their experience, they heard a buzzing in their head. They began to have headaches. They started feeling dizzy. So they have suggested that the aliens are using the tracking devices to keep tabs on humans, rather like us tagging dolphins or birds of prey. Perhaps they're gathering data on our shopping habits. But it's a funny thing about those implants – nobody's ever seen one. The person is always reabducted and the device removed, just in time. Some UFO books will tell you that foreign objects have occasionally shown up on X rays, but don't believe everything you read. Most of these accounts are suspect.

Another theory of why the aliens are here is very creepy, but for some reason, it's also the most popular. Perhaps some people just like to scare themselves with yucky ideas. In any event, this theory has a lot of admirers.

If you recall, Betty Hill reported that the aliens had inserted a probe into her stomach. A few abductees, however, go one better. They claim they were implanted with an alien embryo. And the reason...? Actually, two reasons have been offered. Take your pick.

Choice A: The aliens are here because their race is dying out. Unable to boost their numbers, they've decided it's better to mix their genes with ours than to hold out for purity and go down the tubes. Biologists, however, tell us that differing species cannot interbreed. So this theory is beyond unlikely. It's impossible.

Choice B: Lucky us! Earthlings have been chosen to be foster 'pre-mums'. We carry the alien embryos for a month or two. Then, before anybody knows what's happened, the aliens take them back. This, of course, requires a reabduction. Nobody knows why the aliens are using us in this way, but most people agree it doesn't sound

WHY US?

Books

Arnold, Nick. *Space, Stars and Slimy Aliens* (Horrible Science) Scholastic, 2008.

Bartram, Simon. *Bob's Alien Spotter Guide* Templar Publishing, 2006.

Donkin, Andrew. *Alien Encyclopedia* Collins Voyager, 2002.

Jeffrey, Gary. *UFOs: Alien Abduction and Close Encounters* (Graphic Mysteries), Book House, 2006.

Strong, Jeremy. *I'm Telling You They're Aliens* Puffin Books, 2000.

We6sites

The Royal Observatory
http://www.nmm.ac.uk/server/show/nav.3554
Use this website to learn more about the planets in our solar system and find out more about Earth

NASA (The North American Space Agency)
http://www.nasa.gov/home/
On NASA's website you can learn about America's missions into space and find out about their exploration of the planets.

Film

ET – The Extra Terrestrial. Universal, 1982. DVD.
In this family friendly story an alien meets a boy named Eliot, who then helps his new friend 'ET' to 'phone home' and be reunited with his family .

Batteries not Included. Universal, 1987. DVD.
A group of friends are working to save the block of flats they live in. They are very happy when a group of flying saucers arrive and decide to help.

>> About the Author

Born in Baltimore, Maryland, USA, Judith Herbst grew up in Queens, New York, where she learned to jump double skipping ropes with amazing skill. She has since lost that ability. A former English teacher, she ran away from school to become a writer. Her first book for children was *Sky Above and Worlds Beyond,* whose title, she admits, was much too long. She loves to write and would rather be published, she says, than be rich, which has turned out to be the case. Herbst spends her summers in Maine on a lake with her cats and laptop.

>> Photo-Acknowledgements

Photographs and illustrations in this book are used with the permission of: Fortean Picture Library, pp 6, 8, 9, 10, 11, 12, 13, 16, 17, 19, 23 (Lisa Anders), 24 (Robert Irving), 25 (all), 26 (Debbie Lee), 30, 35 (Dennis Stacy), 41; © Hulton-Deutsch Collection/ CORBIS, p 20; Book cover from COMMUNION: A TRUE STORY by WHITLEY STRIEBER. COPYRIGHT © 1987 BY WILSON AND NEFF, INC. Reprinted by permission of HarperCollins Publishers Inc. WILLIAM MORROW, p 36; © Mark Peterson/CORBIS SABA, p 39; The Wisconsin Center for Film and Theater Research, p 44. Illustrations by Bill Hauser, pp 4-5, 28, 31, 32, 38.

Cover illustration by Bill Hauser.